小李的農曆新年

Li's Chinese New Year

Fang Wang
Illustrated by Jennifer Corfield

Cantonese translation by Sylvia Denham

MANTRA
LINGUA

在農曆新年前的一個星期，小李的全班同學都看了一段有關中國新年巡遊的影片，內有帶著又巨大又色彩繽紛的獅子面具的舞蹈員，跟隨著音樂舞獅助興。

The week before Chinese New Year, Li's class watched a film of a New Year's parade in China. There were lion dancers carrying the huge mask of a colourful lion, making it move with the music.

「我們將會有一個特別為慶祝中國農曆新年的聚會，」
格連老師說：「我想你們在十二生肖中選擇一隻你喜歡的動物，
造一個該動物的面具。」
小李最喜歡造面具。簡老師將薄縐紙及閃亮的卡紙遞給
各個兒童帶回家去 － 但是小李造那一隻動物呢？

"We're having a special assembly to celebrate Chinese New Year,"
said Miss Green. "I'd like each of you to make a mask of your
favourite animal from the Chinese zodiac."
Li loved making masks. Miss Khan gave out tissue paper and shiny
card for the children to take home — but what animal would Li make?

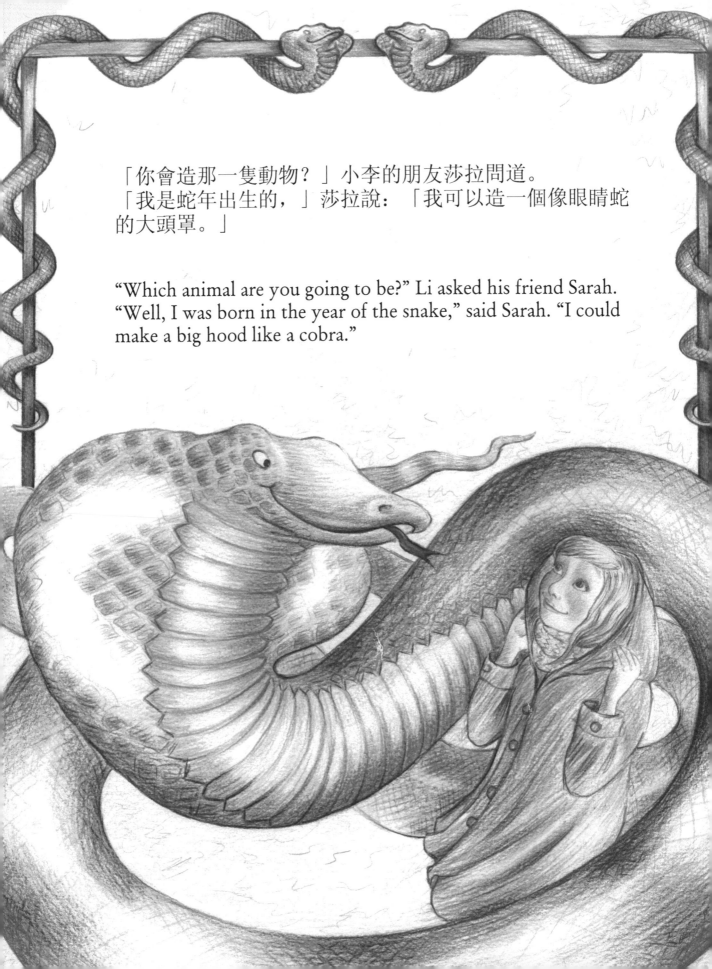

「你會造那一隻動物？」小李的朋友莎拉問道。
「我是蛇年出生的，」莎拉說：「我可以造一個像眼睛蛇的大頭罩。」

"Which animal are you going to be?" Li asked his friend Sarah. "Well, I was born in the year of the snake," said Sarah. "I could make a big hood like a cobra."

可是小李的全班同學中有一半是屬蛇的，他想造與別不同的面具。
「你可以造一個像我的狗樂奇的狗面具。」莎拉笑道。
樂奇擡頭用溫柔的棕色眼睛看著小李。小李肯定他一定會想到更有
趣的動物造他的新年面具的。

But half of Li's class were snakes. He wanted to be something different.
"Well you could be a dog like Lucky," Sarah laughed.
Lucky looked up at Li with soppy, brown eyes. Li was sure he could
find a more exciting animal for his New Year mask.

「你可以造龍啊。」媽媽建議說，
她正在掛貼紅色的賀年揮春。
「一條又大又紅的龍會驅走邪魔，
並會帶來好運。如果在很多年前，
人們沒有造一條巨龍和燃放爆竹，
驅走惡魔連安，現在便沒有中國農曆新年了！」

"Perhaps you could be a dragon," suggested Mum, as she hung the red New Year's banners. "A big, red dragon would scare away bad spirits and bring good luck. There wouldn't even be a Chinese New Year if people hadn't made a huge dragon and let off fireworks to scare away the monster Nian, many years ago!"

「但我在今年的學校遊行中扮龍啊，我不想小李跟我一樣。」
小李的哥哥阿振說。

「我才不想扮龍呢。」小李說，可是他心中卻感到有點失望。

「你可以扮猴子－那麼你就根本不需要面具了。」阿振低聲說道，
以防媽媽聽到。

"But I'm going to be a dragon in the school parade and I don't want
Li copying me — as usual," said Li's big brother Chen.
"I don't want to be a dragon anyway," said Li, although secretly he
was a bit disappointed.
"You can be a monkey — then you won't need a mask at all," Chen
said under his breath so that Mum couldn't hear.

「我或者扮一頭又大又壯的牛，」小李不理會他的哥哥，
「我們即將出生的表弟會屬牛的。」
「除非他是在除夕前出世，否則他會像我一樣，
是一隻老虎 – 最好的動物呢！」
「我才不會造一個笨老虎面具。」小李怒道。

"Maybe I'll be a big, strong ox," said Li, ignoring his brother. "Our new cousin's going to be an ox."
"Only if it's born before New Year's Eve. Otherwise it'll be a tiger like me — the best animal!"
"Well I'm not going to make a stupid tiger mask," said Li crossly.

「別再爭執了，來幫我吧。」媽媽在門廳喊道：「祖母從中國寄來一些美麗的燈籠和剪紙。小李，你能把它們掛起嗎？」
她將一把掃把遞給阿振。「我們還要將整間屋打掃乾淨，把霉氣掃走。」
「噢，媽媽，我一定要做嗎？」阿振哼聲道。

"Stop arguing and come and help me," Mum called from the hall.
"Granny has sent beautiful lanterns and paper cutouts all the way from China. Can you put them up, Li?"
She handed Chen a broom, "And we've got to sweep the whole house to clear away bad luck."
"Oh Mum, do I have to?" Chen groaned.

農曆新年除夕終於來臨， 外公也來了。
他坐在他最喜歡的椅子上，給小李和阿振說
大競賽的故事。

New Year's Eve arrived, and so did Grandpa.
He sat in his favourite chair and told Li and Chen
the story of the great race.

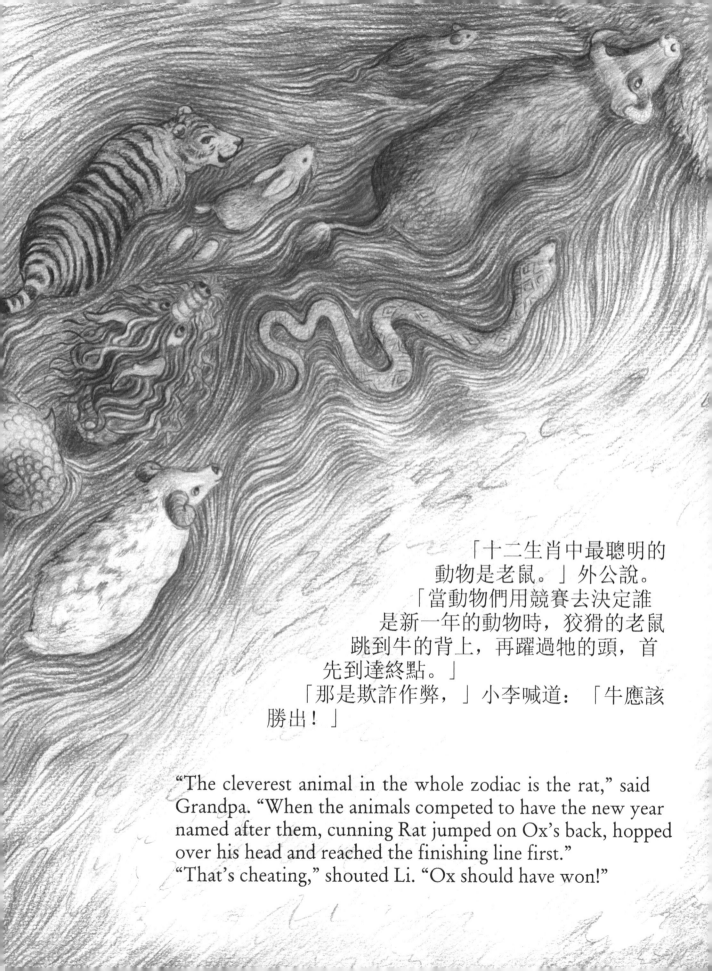

「十二生肖中最聰明的動物是老鼠。」外公說。
「當動物們用競賽去決定誰是新一年的動物時，狡猾的老鼠跳到牛的背上，再躍過牠的頭，首先到達終點。」
「那是欺詐作弊，」小李喊道：「牛應該勝出！」

"The cleverest animal in the whole zodiac is the rat," said Grandpa. "When the animals competed to have the new year named after them, cunning Rat jumped on Ox's back, hopped over his head and reached the finishing line first."
"That's cheating," shouted Li. "Ox should have won!"

「外公，你是屬甚麼動物的？」阿振問道。
「我當然是老鼠！勤奮和可愛 – 我們屬鼠的都有最好的性格。」
「外婆是屬甚麼的？」小李問道。
「她是屬兔的，」外公黯然微笑道：「仁慈、端莊、柔雅。」
「你想她嗎？」小李問道。

"What animal are you Grandpa?" asked Chen.
"I'm a rat, of course! Hardworking and charming — we rats have all the best qualities."
"What animal was Grandma?" asked Li.
"She was a rabbit," Grandpa said, with a sad smile, "kind, graceful and elegant."
"Do you miss her?" Li asked.

「那是一個愚蠢的問題。」阿振說。

「不，那是一個很好的問題，」外公說：「我很掛念她，並想告訴你們有關她的事，我會在年初三想念親人的那天告訴你們更多有關她的往事。」

媽媽在門口說：「你們兩個來，是包餃子的時候了。」

"That's a silly question," said Chen.

"No, it's a good question," said Grandpa. "I miss her very much, and I like to talk about her. I'll tell you more about her on the third day of Chinese New Year when we remember loved ones."

Mum appeared in the doorway. "Okay, you two, it's time to make some dumplings."

爸爸和媽媽一大早便已經忙碌地進進出出廚房。當小李看到為晚上準備的各種不同的菜餚時，他的肚子便隆隆作響，有肉丸子、雞絲、魚條和饅頭，羊肉卷看來十分可口。

Mum and Dad had been in and out of the kitchen since very early in the morning. Li's stomach growled when he saw all the different dishes ready for the evening. There were meatballs, chicken and fish strips, and steamed bread. The lamb rolls looked delicious.

媽媽把肉餡和麵粉糰拿出來，快速地將一些肉餡包成球狀，小李想模仿她，可是他的餃子總是包成各種大小不同的形狀。
「沒關係，」媽媽說：「它們會一樣的好吃。現在先閉上眼睛。」她偷偷地將一枚硬幣放進一隻餃子中。

Mum brought out the meat stuffing and flour. She quickly shaped some stuffing into a neat ball. Li tried to copy her, but his dumplings were all shapes and sizes. "Don't worry," said Mum, "they'll taste just as good. Now close your eyes," and she slipped a coin into one of the dumplings.

「各位，恭喜發財！」爸爸在晚餐時說。

「新年快樂！」小李和阿振齊叫道。

小李一直吃到肚子都快要撐爆了。「最好的生肖動物或者就是能吃得最多的動物。」他建議說。

「最吃得的可能是豬。」媽媽說。

小李聽到阿振嗤嗤地笑，於是便決定不造豬的面具。

「有些人相信每一年都是依據十二生肖中的其中一隻動物而命名，那是因爲牠們有出席皇帝的宴會。」爸爸說：「其他的動物也有被邀請，但是牠們因爲太懶惰而沒有去。」

小李突然看到他的餃子裏面有閃亮的東西。

「我找到幸運錢幣啊。」他叫道。

"Kung Hei Fat Choi, everyone!" said Dad at dinner that evening.

"Happy New Year!" shouted Li and Chen.

Li ate until he thought he would burst. "Maybe the best animal is the one that can eat the most," he suggested.

"The biggest eater is probably the pig," said Mum.

Li heard Chen giggle and decided not to make a pig mask.

"Well, some people believe that the twelve zodiac animals each had a year named after them for attending the emperor's feast," said Dad. "The other animals were all invited, but they were too lazy to make the journey."

Suddenly Li noticed something shiny in his dumpling. "I found the lucky coin," he cried.

晚飯後，一家人穿得暖暖的，一起到公園去觀看新年的慶祝會。

After dinner, the family wrapped up warm and went to the park to watch the New Year's celebrations.

小李的朋友莎拉和她的爸爸媽媽也在那裏，他們一起看壯觀的舞龍和精彩的煙花匯演。
小李肯定他在煙花中可以看到十二生肖中的一些動物，但是他真的能看到嗎？

Li's friend Sarah was there with her mum and dad, and together they watched the spectacular dragon dances and the fantastic firework display.
Li was sure he could see some of the animals from the Chinese zodiac in the fireworks, but he couldn't really, could he?

第二天是年初一，是新年的元旦日。小李在床上看到新衣服，那都是特別為象徵新開始而買的。

「起來，懶骨頭！我們去給爸爸媽媽拜年！」他一邊說，一邊跳到阿振的床上去。

「你應該是屬公雞的，」阿振說：「有你在這裏，誰會需要鬧鐘啊！」

The next day was Kalends, the first day of the New Year. Li found new clothes on his bed, bought specially to represent new beginnings.

"Wake up, sleepyhead! Let's go and wish Mum and Dad a Happy New Year!" he said, jumping on the end of Chen's bed.

"You should be a rooster," Chen said, yawning. "Who needs an alarm clock with you around!"

在早餐時，媽媽拿出兩個印有金字的紅封包，把一個給阿振，一個給小李。紅封包內的錢幣合算起來是雙數的 － 一個幸運的象徵。
「我們有好消息，」媽媽說。小李正在計劃如何用他的利是錢。
「你們有一個新表妹 － 美芬和泰舅父有一個新嬰孩。」

At breakfast, Mum took out two small red packets covered with golden words, one for Chen and one for Li. The coins in each packet added up to an even number: a lucky sign.

"There's more good news too," said Mum, as Li planned what to do with his money. "You have a new cousin — Mei-Fen and Uncle Tai have a new baby."

「那麼它是屬老虎抑或牛呢？」阿振問。
「*她*是一個小女孩，」媽媽說：「她是牛年最後的幾分鐘出生的。」
「我就知道她會是屬牛的。」小李笑著臉說。

"So is it a tiger or an ox then?" asked Chen.
"*She* is a little girl," said Mum, "and she was born in the last few minutes of the year of the ox."
"I knew she'd be an ox," said Li, with a big smile.

小李並不在乎他的表妹的生肖是甚麼，不過他仍然不知道造甚麼生肖動物的面具。他嘗試造了幾個，但是沒有一個造得好。
「別灰心，小李，」爸爸說：「看看外公帶了甚麼來。」
外公拿著兩個精美的動物風箏。

Li didn't really mind what animal his cousin was. And he still didn't know what mask to make. He had tried to make a few, but none turned out right.
"Cheer up, Li," said Dad. "Look what Grandpa has brought."
Grandpa was carrying two beautiful, animal-shaped kites.

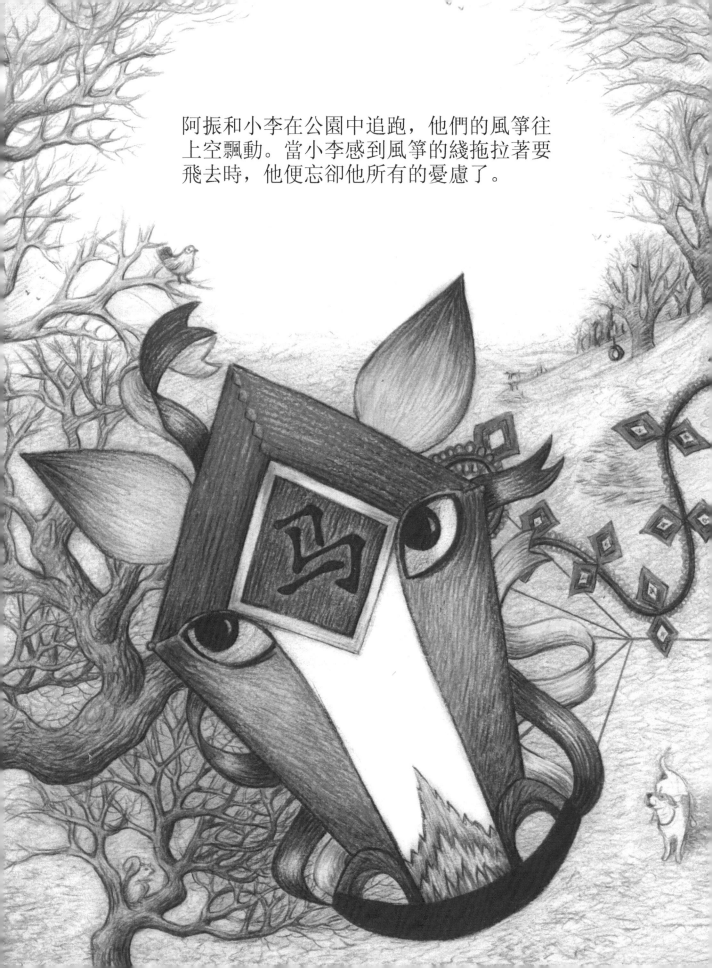

阿振和小李在公園中追跑，他們的風箏往上空飄動。當小李感到風箏的綫拖拉著要飛去時，他便忘卻他所有的憂慮了。

Chen and Li raced through the park with their new kites soaring above them. Li forgot about his worries as he felt the kite tugging on the string, trying to fly away.

第二天上學前，小李感到憂慮不安，他實在很想參加學校的聚會。
然而，不能決定造甚麼面具的就不僅是他一個。

Before school the next day, Li felt sad. He really wanted to be in the
school assembly. But he wasn't the only one who couldn't decide what
mask to make.

在休息時，小李、達力、積克和森米娜都走去跟格連老師傾談。
「不用擔心，」她說：「我有最好的安排。我需要幾位自願者在
聚會中做一些特別的事情，我們已經有很多可愛的中國生肖動物，
但是… 」

At break time, Li, Tariq, Jack and Samira all went to talk to Miss Green.
"Don't worry," she said, "I have the perfect plan. I need some volunteers
for an extra special part of the assembly. We already have lots of lovely
Chinese zodiac animals, but..."

「⋯我們仍需要一些人去舞龍啊！」

"...we still need some dragon dancers!"

鼠
Rat
2008
Charming
Popular
▶

Ox
2009
Patient
Logical
▶

龙
Dragon
2012
Energetic
Confident
▶

蛇
Snake
2013
Thoughtful
Wise
▶

猴
Monkey
2016
Ambitious
Cheeky
▶

鸡
Rooster
2017
Idealistic
Honest
▶

虎
Tiger
2010
Romantic
Brave
▶

兔
Rabbit
2011
Lucky
Tidy
▶

马
Horse
2014
Dynamic
Cheerful
▶

羊
Ram
2015
Sincere
Artistic
▶

狗
Dog
2018
Alert
Loyal
▶

猪
Pig
2019
Happy
Outspoken
▶

MASK MAKING

paints
brush
pen
scissors
card
string
paper plate
tape

choose your character

Tiger

Rabbit

Dragon

Use your Talking Pen to choose a character then follow the 3 stages of instructions to make a mask and celebrate your chosen year.

Tiger 2010   Rabbit 2011   Dragon 2012

Stage 1 ▶

Stage 2 ▶

Stage 3 ▶

■ Story mode

Origins of the Chinese Zodiac

▷   ▷   ▷

3184050